CO

Introduction ....

Module 1 - Learning

So, my child is 'Sensitive', what does it mean exactly?
So how are these people different and what does "highly sensitive "mean?
Is every sensitive person/child the same?
Sensitive? Empath? Intuitive? Introvert? Shy? What's the difference?
Why is my child sensitive?
But still; why is my child sensitive?
Do genetics play a part?
Is this Highly Sensitive Person thing new?
How can I balance understanding and compassion with behavior management? Explaining it to others

Module 1 - Learning that your child is sensitive ....
Part 2

How can I help my child?
Practice Understanding
Empathize
Calm and Protect
But how do I handle a meltdown?!

Module 2 - Managing a sensitives child's Lifestyle ....

Why is lifestyle/environment important?
When do your child's sensitivities increase
and become un-manageable? Noticing
and adapting. Notice, notice, notice
Adapt, Adapt, Adapt
Check in with your child's timetable
Clear schedules and making time for downtime.
So, what can I do?
This sounds all a bit boring!
A word about you…

Module 3 - Cleanse and Calm. ....

Energy
<u>Cleansing techniques</u>
Salt Baths
Cleansing & protecting Sprays
Sage/Palo Santo
Crystals
<u>Calming Techniques</u>
Breathing techniques
How to develop slow and gentle breathing:
Grounding
Hand Mudra Technique
Relaxing Body Scan
Worry monster and Fairy doors
Essential Oils
Having a good cry
<u>Protection Techniques</u>

- Crystals
- Protective sprays
- Invoking a protection bubble - Visualisation - But what if…?

Module 4 - Empower & Thrive. ....

Empower
Don't see it as a weakness!!
Owning sensitivity
Sensitive superpower
Talk about it
Thrive
Hobbies and Opportunities
Communication
Last word
Reflection
The Future
Other resources

**<u>You are not permitted to reproduce, copy or republish this
material without prior
consent or permission.</u>
Thank you**

Kathryn Pearson © 2017   www.kathrynpearson.co.uk

Introduction

You're here because you worry about your child fitting into this world and you worry that they will miss out in life because of *how they are.*

You get frustrated with their behavior and you don't know how to handle their strong emotional reactions.

You fear that won't ever reach their potential because they're "sensitive".

You've heard about children being "sensitive" or "empathic" and you want to learn more.

You're here because you don't buy into the labels that are being branded about. According to one scientific website, I'm likely to have a "sensory processing disorder" because of my sensitive traits - nope, not me. I don't have a "disorder" - and you're here because you feel that way too.

You're here because you desperately want to help your child be the best person they can be, celebrating their uniqueness and you want to help to empower them.

You're also here because you're an AMAZING parent!

And I want to thank you for that: being here and being willing to invest time and money into learning how you can be parenting your amazing sensitive child in a way that will nurture and empower them to THRIVE!

I'm excited to take this journey with you and introduce you to the world of a sensitive child - you see I was one and I now have one ;)

Seen as the Highly Sensitive thing is relatively new to you, I thought you would have LOADS of questions. I've summarized the most common ones about discovering High Sensitivity in this first chapter. The following chapters or "modules" move onto:

- Lifestyle - how to manage your child's schedule to reduce overwhelm and meltdowns
- The importance of downtime and clear spaces
- Cleansing your (empathic) highly sensitive space and energy
- Calming techniques for highly sensitive children
- Protection strategies for sensitives & empaths
- Discovering, nurturing and empowering your sensitive's superpowers!!

This eBook has been created out of my desire to help other parents of sensitive children; being a parent of one myself. **But more importantly than that, I too was a highly sensitive child.**

My Mother is amazing – absolutely amazing. But she had no idea I was a Highly Sensitive Person, specifically an Intuitive Sensitive.

She knew I was "sensitive", yes, but in the early 80's the term "Highly Sensitive Person" didn't exist. I was deemed to be a bit of a wimp in my family. As an only child, I was constantly compared to my cousins who had siblings and therefore were tougher and more rough and tumble than me, naturally. My Mum tried to toughen me up – but it didn't work.

I'm still as sensitive now as I was back then. She struggled with what the rest of the family thought of me and what they thought of how she parented me. She got frustrated with my melt downs and how I would only wear one particular polo shirt (it was the comfiest!) She struggled to understand why I had these meltdowns and outburst of strong emotions.

She was bemused at my level of sensitivity to noise - every night insisting she only had the TV on Volume #15 and NO louder.

I struggled to feel understood. I struggled to communicate how I felt and I generally struggled with fitting in - anywhere. I couldn't toughen up no matter how hard I tried, I had this bubble of emotions always present at the surface, ready to explode whenever I was triggered. Crying in public was commonplace. I was an easy target.

I went through life thinking there was **fundamentally something wrong with me.**

I didn't discover about my Highly Sensitive nature until I was 30 years old. It changed my life overnight – I don't want other children to have to wait this long and struggle like I did; missing out on the fun in life, being and feeling misunderstood by relatives, peers and strangers, not reaching their full potential (not even getting close) and having strained relationships with their nearest and dearest.

I want you to be able to talk to your children about being sensitive.

I want them to be able to come to you with their problems.

I want you to be able to help and support your sensitive child.

I want to help you to fully understand them and why they react the way they do.

I want to help you and your child to avoid "melt-downs" at all costs.

I want the world to know and understand just how amazingly brilliant sensitive people are, and I want us to feel valued and worthy!

So that, in a nutshell, is why I'm here writing this Book. It's been within me for so long and I'm bursting with pride and joy now it's finally here.

I hope you enjoy reading and learning as much as I loved getting it all down on paper for you.

I want to constantly support my readers, so please connect with me on:

Instagram: @kathryn_pearson_
Facebook: Kathryn Pearson EFT
Email kathrynpearsoneft@gmail.com

Facebook Group
Please join "The Sensitive Subject" Facebook Group

If you're still unsure if your child is sensitive or not you can find Dr E Arons High Sensitive Person questionnaire at www.hsperson.com

It's my plea that you see the simplicity and beauty of parenting a highly sensitive child. It's not an illness or a disorder. Your child isn't broken and there is no label you must accept. Sensitivity is not a label - merely a personality trait. I'm sensitive, but I'm also confident, outgoing, introverted, determined and super friendly and caring/empathic, and I hope you learn you manage your child's sensitive traits so that they can thrive with it integrated into the full expression of who they are too.

Disclaimer: I am not a medical professional, nor claim to be. The information and activities contained within this Book are for informational purposes and should be used at your own discretion. It should not replace any medical intervention, if you have concerns about your child's physical, emotional or mental health please speak to a medical professional or GP

Module 1
Learning that your child is sensitive

So, my child is 'Sensitive', what does it mean exactly?

Firstly, your child, as all children are, is amazing. You may have multiple children, one who is more sensitive than the other, or even in different ways.

A sensitive child is no better or worse than any other child - they simply have a different personality trait. One which means they notice more about their environment.

The term 'highly sensitive person' was developed by Dr Elaine Aron in the mid-90s, and she estimates that around 15-20% of the population are Highly Sensitive people.

So how are these people different from the rest of the population and what does "highly sensitive "mean?

Elaine Aron defines high sensitivity individuals as:

> *"...those born with a tendency to notice more in their environment and deeply reflect on everything before acting.."*

They notice more because they have more sensitive nervous systems than non-sensitives, which means their sensory processing is heightened - meaning they see, feel, hear, process, observe and sense way more sensory stuff than other people. They notice the details.

Sensory stimulus includes:
- Tastes,
- Smells,
- Sight and visual information,
- Hearing,
- Touch and textures, including mouth feel, and - Feelings & emotions.

They may also have a strong intuition and a strong sense of empathy towards others.

As a general example:

A sensitive child walks into a busy classroom; they first pick up on the visual overload: the brightly colored displays, the tone and brightness of the lighting, where the windows are and how much natural light is coming in.

They will notice the new funny smells of the classroom, and how the smells make them feel. They notice the layers and layers of different noises coming from every corner of the room; the children's voices, the adult conversations, the screechy squeak of the chairs being pushed back to sit on. They may still be feeling, and maybe irritated by, the itchy and scratchy uniform they have been forced to wear, that their socks feel funny in their shoes, and that their hair doesn't feel right.

They will also notice the invisible 'feeling' or atmosphere of the room. They will sense if their teacher likes them or not, they will sense who is happy and who is sad.

This is not irregular or abnormal for them; life has always been this way; it's completely normal to notice this much.

All this information will be coming to them at the same time.

Kathryn Pearson © 2017   www.kathrynpearson.co.uk

They will be processing all this information via their Central Nervous System; messages and signals shooting between the senses and the brain. Detail upon detail will be processed and relayed - all day long.

Can you imagine how that must feel?

Being a Highly Sensitive person myself I can't tell you how overwhelming it is. I can barely have a conversation in a classroom situation like the one above, it feels as though I can't concentrate, but really, my sensory system is processing too much information to be able to talk as well. It takes a HUGE AMOUNT of strength and energy to be able to block it out and focus.

This isn't to say that your child won't ever learn to be resilient in this situation; but for little ones starting school, for example, it can be like this.

A highly sensitive child (or person) notices more information from the world around them via their senses - they are also likely to be in tune with other people's emotions, and some can empathise with others and maybe even sense when something's not right.

It is a personality trait and when it is well managed and understood your child will thrive.

Kathryn Pearson © 2017   www.kathrynpearson.co.uk

But when it's not the HS person can feel overwhelmed, misunderstood, frustrated, exhausted, weepy and anxious...

Being a Highly Sensitive Person is not a burden (although it sounds like one!) they don't need to be toughened up. I can't tell you how much a sensitive person just longs to be understood, and empathised with.

Is every sensitive person/child the same?

Absolutely not!

Each sensitive person has their own unique finger print and levels of different sensitivities.

Me? I'm all about sound and feeling. I can hear the buzzing of the clock on the microwave, I physically get repulsed at fuzzy radios. I can sense when something's not right and know how others feel. I can't bear shopping centers and supermarkets makes me feel sick. (Don't get me wrong, I still go to them, but I feel totally fuzzed out afterwards.) My heart is always on my sleeve and no matter how hard people have tried; I cannot be toughened up.

But I really hear people, I can listen and feel what's going on. I'm empathic and deeply caring; wanting to help. My intuitive sense makes me an awesome teacher, because I can hold space and adapt my teaching exactly to the needs of my students

My daughter on the other hand is sensitive to how things feel on her skin - itchy labels, socks feeling funny and visual stuff - too much visual stimulation can cause over tiredness and irritability. She spent the first year of her life observing everything. No desire to crawl or walk or even roll over - just observe and take it in.

But she really sees what goes on. She's great to have around when siblings fall out :) She's an observer - and we don't know yet where this will take her, but I know it will be a skill which will set her apart.

I also know children who get overwhelmed with social situations because of their sensitivity. Some who are very sensitive to tastes and mouth textures. Some who are so in tune with how others feel, they find it hard to connect to their own inner needs, putting how others feel before themselves. Some who are deeply connected to the world around them - plants, flowers, bugs and insects - they couldn't care less about making friends, and some who are so incredibly emotionally sensitive; maybe getting upset when others do or being scared of loud children but caring deeply about other children and always wanting to help.

Kathryn Pearson © 2017   www.kathrynpearson.co.uk

I'm pretty hopeful you can relate to one of these examples?

Each child has their own unique variations of sensitivity. Their own unique fingerprint. Their own identity. Their own Sensitive superpower!

But right now maybe that superpower feels more like a weakness?

This guide is designed to help you understand them and empower you to help your child to thrive as a sensitive person.

It is not something they need to turn off or toughen up to.

Your child is uniquely brilliantly sensitive + empathic in their own special way and they chose you to help you nurture that superpower!

The world needs them.

Sensitive? Empath? Intuitive? Introvert? Shy? What's the difference?

Well, there are certainly blurred lines around the terms. Let's define each one to see if that helps:

A Highly Sensitive Person, as we know means: "…those born with a tendency to notice more in their environment and deeply reflect on everything before acting.." *Dr E. Aron. The Highly Sensitive Child.* They have more sensitive nervous systems. They also can be deeply empathic and intuitive.

An Empath, is described as someone who: "…is affected by other people's energies and that have an innate ability to intuitively feel and perceive others.

Empaths can process other people's feelings and energy…and can take on the emotions of other people." Christel Broederlow (www.themindunleased.com/2013/10/30-traits-of-an-empath.html)

A person can be both Highly Sensitive and an Empath. Personally, I think the two are very closely linked, and it's likely that your child shows signs of being both emphatic and sensitive. As an empath + HS person myself I've found that these people can also **learn** to be very closed off and protect themselves from other people's energies. But they don't always learn this!

Empaths or Highly Sensitive People can also be Intuitive.

Intuitive, defined by the Oxford English Dictionary, is a word used to describe some one's ability to use what a person feels to be true, rather than relying on conscious reasoning - instinctive. They know, they feel, they don't need evidence - they just know.

Again, your child may show signs of being intuitive too.

An introvert, on the other hand is described by Oxford English Dictionary, as a person predominantly concerned with their own thoughts and feelings rather than with external things, a shy, reticent person.

Which to me sounds like a Sensitive person in hiding!

So, overwhelmed with their inner world and sensory external overload, they *become introverted* as a protection mechanism. How do you feel about those definitions? Where does your child sit within those definitions?

Hopefully you can see there is a lot of crossover. I certainly cross over these definitions, for example. I have always been sensitive, deeply empathic, and very intuitive - but life's harsh lessons made me hide these traits and ignore them. Frustrated, anxious, nervous and a very, very stressed adult, it wasn't until I read Heidi Sawyers Book "Highly Intuitive People" that I understood who I was - what kind of personality I really had. I highly recommend her book if you feel that you or your child is intuitive as well as Highly Sensitive and you want to research this topic even further.

This eBook and the following chapters contain information which can be used to help these different types of people. If I know where to find more information about a certain topic, I will recommend it throughout the text. I've tried to summarise everything I can, so that you get the facts and the important information - I know how little time you have!

It's really special when you start to really know yourself; when you can confidently and proudly say "I'm sensitive but I'm also empathic too".

Try to help your child to understand where they sit within these definitions, by knowing them yourself. I believe we should all know who we are, rather than being told what we are by other people.

People might tell your child they are "shy" or "quiet" or even worse "good".
They may learn that they are "emotional" or "too soft".
They might even start to think that these things are bad!

It's your job to strengthen your child's inner power with the facts about who they really are - strengthening their self-awareness and developing a confident sense of identity.

We do this by understanding the definitions our self-first, and then teaching them to our children. We do it by challenging family members and correcting peoples "harmless" comments about who and what our children are.

A wise friend once said to me "No one else will stick up for your children, you have to fight their corner each and every step of the way!"

Do people try and put labels on your children? Whose comments hurt the most? Where does your child sit within these definitions and how to do you feel about that? How do you perceive "sensitive" people or "shy" people? And why? Could this be affecting your relationship or your ability to empathise with your child?

Kathryn Pearson © 2017   www.kathrynpearson.co.uk

Why is my child sensitive?

I'm not like this - so why is my child? They must have got it from their Grandmother/Dad - or is it me? Am I sensitive too?

I can empathise with you - our children's sensitive personality traits can be totally alien to us, even if we are sensitive too, and as much as you adore your child, a part of you longs to understand why your child is sensitive and where they are going to fit into the world.

To help do this, let's go to the animal kingdom. Elaine Aron states that numerous species of animal have been found to have members of their groups to be more 'sensitive and cautious' than others.

This diversity in animal populations has meant that they survive and they have been able to keep evolving and thrive. Their differences in personality has allowed this.

Dr Aron uses the example of a group of deer. It has been observed that within a herd of deer, some are more sensitive and cautious than others, and for very good reasons.

For example; a group of deer come to a clearing in the woods with luscious green grass. Some of the deer do a quick check and then head straight out and start eating the luscious, life-sustaining grass, knowing that if they don't eat the grass now, they could die of malnourishment, their babies would go un-fed and they wouldn't be strong enough to flee a predator.

Whereas, some hang back, much more cautious, knowing that if they rush out and start eating the lush grass a predator or hunter could be lurking and they could be killed instantly, this too being a threat to their survival and the survival of their family group. They check and check again, using all their relevant senses (smell, hearing, sight, intuition) to make sure it's safe before proceeding.

Now for this species of animal to survive - BOTH types of deer are needed - the more bold one and the more cautious one. If all the deer were as bold as the first one, the entire herd could be wiped out instantly.

Whereas if the entire herd were as cautious and sensitive, the herd may never get the nutrition to survive.

It is the same with humans - both types are needed for our society to thrive.

Your child is a vital member of society and the world, and they need understanding, compassion and the knowledge to be able to thrive in our modern
"Sensitive Un-Friendly" world.

Kathryn Pearson © 2017   www.kathrynpearson.co.uk

For so long, our world has been ruled by the un-sensitive. Which has served evolution and us well thus far.

However, to the brilliantly amazing sensitives who are emerging (as teachers, healers, doctors, inventors, scientists, change makers, environmentalists) our modern-day world is just too much.

Most of everything in our modern society is too much for them - spending time at busy indoor play centers, with their bright colors and funny noises, busy school environments, with lots of other children energies, problems and issues to solve, increasing amounts of technology, busy large shopping centers, with the bright lights, vast, vast amounts of people and noises and smells, the schedules of their parents, busy, busy lifestyles, little down-time or outdoor play, rushing around, homework, processed food, the list could go on…

But still; why is my child sensitive?

In short: The world needs them. Modern lifestyles are killing us. Modern lifestyles are killing the planet. Un-sensitive, push, push, push mindsets are becoming less appealing as we all move back to noticing what's really important:

Love, family, experiences, enjoyment, fulfillment and happiness.

Kathryn Pearson © 2017   www.kathrynpearson.co.uk

There is a shift and your child is of the generation that will help facilitate, design and move this shift forward.

- **How does this feel?**
- **Do you agree that things are changing?**
- **How can you see your child helping the world?**
- **What are their interested or talents?**
- **How can you celebrate and nurture these?**

Do genetics play a part?

Science and research would suggest yes, to some extent. It can be an inherited gene, however it doesn't matter too much, you don't need to agonise over why they are sensitive.

Your sensitive child is a gift, and no doubt that gift is teaching you more about yourself than you ever imagined!

Is this Highly Sensitive Person thing new?

Personally, I think sensitive people have always been around - however before they were labeled introverts, or anxious, maybe they would isolate themselves from society. They may have been branded weak or sensitive, eccentric even?!

In 1913, Carl Jung (highly influential psychiatrist and psychotherapist), first mentioned the concept of "innate sensitiveness" in some of his lectures. He proposed that some people are born more sensitive than others.

Dr Elaine Aron (who is a "Jungarian" Psychotherapist) conducted extensive research in the 90's and has since written and published many bestselling books on the topic. Heidi Sawyer has written and published the book "Highly Intuitive People".

So, the answer is probably yes, it is a relatively new thing and isn't understood or accepted by everyone. However, by you reading this, talking about it and sharing your new knowledge with others, awareness will spread!

How can I balance understanding and compassion with behavior management?

This is possibly the most tricky part of the whole journey, and I think I can only suggest a personal approach! Managing my daughter's behavior whilst being understanding and compassionate has caused me hurdles and problems for sure.

My husband isn't half as understanding or empathic to her, yet he gets all the good behavior, he gets listened to straight away, she does as she's is told when Daddy is around. Which sometimes makes me doubt my empathic approach!

I seem to get it all - the tantrums, the attitude, the rudeness, the meltdowns, the in-depth bed time chats, the sensitive meltdowns and gut wrenching tears. It can be overwhelming and frustrating for me.

But my gut and my heart (and even my head most of the time) tell me that without my understanding and compassion, she wouldn't be nearly as confident or happy as she is.

She knows she's sensitive and I've always been empathic and open with her. She feels understood and this helps her develop a great relationship with a non-sensitive parent (and the sensitive one too!), and ***most importantly develop a sense of identity around who she is and what her needs are.***

This is my personal experience and sometimes I do worry about being "too soft" - but my instincts tell me to be this way. I listen to my instincts because I completely trust them when it comes to parenting - I can feel it in my body. I don't do what I "should" do. I don't follow any rules and have found my own way with a balance of compassion and understanding and behavior management. I recommend you do the same!

We have used the naughty step, reward charts, bribes. We have used shouting, punishments, ignoring. We have tried understanding, compassion, and empathy. At the moment, aged almost 6, my daughter is back on the naughty step as she moves into a stage of seeing how far she can push the boundaries, AGAIN!

And after trying all this, we found what works and what doesn't. And these have changed as she's gotten older.

Shouting and harsh punishments certainly don't work. Being very clear and having boundaries has. Empathy and compassion and understanding also have had a huge impact.

Whatever you chose to do, find your own balance, and know that the way you parent your sensitive and non-sensitive children, maybe different to others.

Explaining it to others

How do I explain this to others? Well, first of all, chose who you tell wisely.

Some people just won't get it, luckily some will! The most important people are their teachers, caregivers and anyone looking after your child in your absence. You can explain it in your own way, show them this eBook, and refer them to blogs or articles you find, or refer them to Elaine's books.

I explained it to my husband using the deer example firstly. I wasn't sure he would get it.

Coincidently, he had watched a programme about animals and he said that they explained something similar! So, he was able to "get it" quicker than I thought he would. Really, it's science and if we go at it from that angle, people are more receptive. High Sensitivity is a personality trait, not a disorder or an illness. Without empathy, sensitivity and cautious behavior, mankind wouldn't survive. Simple.

I feel it's gravely important to speak about Sensitivity and Empathy openly.

I mean, if we don't, it's like it's wrong, or bad, or a weakness that we should be ashamed of. And it's simply not.

Non- sensitive people are not robots; they're still human! And they **are** likely to understand. Be proud and confident with how you explain it!

Kathryn Pearson © 2017   www.kathrynpearson.co.uk

Part 2
Learning that your child is sensitive

How can I help my child?

Just *knowing* that your child is sensitive helps them massively. The next three chapters I will describe in more detail how you can help manage their lifestyle, communicate with them, cleanse their energy and calm them down, protect and empower them.

You *knowing* they are a sensitive means you're on their team; and when they need it most you can understand, empathise, calm, protect and empower them. This is something every sensitive needs. *You just knowing that they are sensitive and what this means will help them in ways you will never know!*

Practice Understanding

Understanding that when they are 'overwhelmed', fussy or hyper sensitive that they're not acting, making it up or just trying to make life awkward for you. *Remember they really do have a sensitive nervous system* and if they are having a particularly busy day, aren't rested or are over stimulated, then they WILL HAVE A MELTDOWN!

Their meltdown is due to the fact they need something and it's a job for both of you to work out what that is - whether it's a calming technique, to cancel the play date, a cuddle in the toilets, an extra dose of empathy or a day of down-time.

Remove yourself from the "energy" of it i.e. don't get caught up in their meltdown. Instead, detach and *know that taking the time to understand what's going on will reduce, in time, the frequency of meltdowns and drama.*

Instead of rolling eyes, or telling them to pull themselves together, or saying "Get a grip, it can't be THAT bad!" (Oh yes, I've said that too!) calmly explain to them that you want to understand - "Mummy wants to understand why you're so upset, Mummy wants to help you. That's my job. So, try your best to use your voice to tell me, so I can help you." Over and over again.

Instead of getting frustrated, feeling like you're the worst parent in the world and reaching for the nearest bottle of wine, take the time to know:

You're not alone.
You're doing the best you can right now.
You're striving to understand them and that massive.
You were meant to be a parent to a sensitive child.

Try to be understanding of their sensitive 'quirks' - rather than dismissing them or letting them become frustrating.

Kathryn Pearson © 2017   www.kathrynpearson.co.uk

If they cry because a child has pushed them over in the soft play, let them cry, be understanding that this situation is in fact, **emotionally painful** and their tears are valid! Understand that their sleeves rolling up under their coat is feels physically repulsive and their reaction is valid!

Understand that it's your job to normalise these kinds of things for them and nurture this sensitivity so that it becomes manageable rather than trying to squash it.

Empathise

Empathise with them! The language you use and your honesty will go miles.

"I can see that you're really upset…. talk to me about it…" or "I can see you're in pain, I know it's really not nice hurting your arm, let's try to work together to see if we can calm you down.."

If you are sensitive yourself you will find this a little easier maybe (I say this, being a sensitive myself, however it isn't always as easy as it sounds - especially if I'm having an overwhelm day or feeling extra sensitive!)

however, even if you're not, put yourself in their shoes; they are noticing and processing more from their environment than other children - making them irritable, upset, tired,

Kathryn Pearson © 2017   www.kathrynpearson.co.uk

moody and even weepy, especially if they are empathic or intuitive too.

I always felt as though no one understood me and I never wanted my child to feel that way too. Really do try to put yourself in their shoes.

Calm and Protect

Chapter three describes strategies and techniques you can use to help calm your sensitive child, and this, combined with empathising and understanding, will go a LONG way to helping them.

It really is so lovely learning how to cleanse and calm your child (and yourself!) with natural and safe products and techniques.

Each child will have their favorites, so I have included a range for you to try. Don't be overwhelmed - just choose the ones that resonate with you.

This chapter also suggests ideas for energetic protection - empaths, sensitives and intuitive people often become 'easy targets' for others, or be easily drained in others company.

Their open personalities, heart on their sleeve and caring nature, can mean they are easily hurt by others. There are lots of protection strategies you can use to strengthen your child, without them losing their sensitive caring nature, empowering them to grow into their sensitive superpowers!

But how do I handle a meltdown?!

Firstly, I want to empower you to apply strategies and techniques to help prevent meltdowns and overly emotional outbursts, so please use and try out the strategies I have outlined in the 2nd and 3rd modules - but inevitably they will still happen from time to time, especially in the early days while you are finding your feet.

So here are my top tips for handling meltdowns:

1. First of all, don't engage! Don't get sucked in. Check in with yourself before you respond (not react!!) Take a breath.
2. Secondly, understand and remember they are having a reaction to being overwhelmed, their sensitive nervous systems are over stimulated, and they are reaching out for help. They need you to understand them!
3. Try your best not to let the judgments of other people affect how you deal with this situation. I know that's hard, I know it's tough, I know it can be embarrassing; but try your absolute best!
4. Empathise. Get down on their level and validate their emotions, but not the behavior: "I can see that you are really upset/angry/excited/sad, and it's OK to be

upset/angry/excited/sad - but it isn't OK to hit mummy/shout/throw etc. I want to understand why you're reacting this way, so please use your words and help me to understand. If you continue *** (name the behavior you don't want to see) then you will have to go on the naughty step/have timeout/not have TV time. But I want to help you - so please talk to me.

5. Then listen.
6. Ask some feeling questions "so how does that make you feel?", "What would make you feel better?"
7. Then listen some more.
8. Understand and empathise the best you can, but if you don't, be honest with them! They can sense in authenticity a mile off!
9. See if you can help them with a practical solution, or simply just validate their feelings. Remember they want to be understood and know that you're on their team and they're not wrong for being "different".
10. Don't let your perceived judgments of other people affect the way you deal with them.
11. Have a cuddle in the toilets and try a calming technique, if you have one. If you're out and about I've found hand washing to be a great way of bringing the benefits of a salt bath (mentioned later) anywhere! So, go wash hands together or wipe them with a baby wipe.
12. Love them hard. And love yourself harder.

Kathryn Pearson © 2017   www.kathrynpearson.co.uk

Module 2
Managing a Sensitive Childs Lifestyle

Kathryn Pearson © 2017 www.kathrynpearson.co.uk

Why is lifestyle/environment important?

In the first module I talked about how your child's sensory system picks up on a huge about of information from the world around them.

Processing this barrage of sensory information, day in, day out, is exhausting.

This exhaustion can cause huge melt downs, introverted behavior, restlessness, angry outbursts, lots of crying, disturbed sleep patterns (not being able to sleep or switch off) and general unhappiness. Which are the results of
OVERWHELM!

It can also impact your relationship with your child and the relationship they have with themselves.

When you don't know that you're sensitive and you try to keep up with the modern world and non-sensitive people, life becomes overwhelming and bewildering.

You start to believe something is wrong with you. You can't keep up; you can't maintain the energy of a non-sensitive. You react differently, and you notice that.

Empathic Sensitive's can't understand why they feel so utterly exhausted and drained after a trip to the shopping center, yet their friends are still laughing, giggling and talking. All they want to do is go home.

Intuitive Sensitive's get confusing and mixed messages from non-sensitive's - feeling and knowing things are wrong but being told the opposite by a non-sensitive person.

Knowing this, it's really our job as parents, to manage their daily experiences and lifestyle to reduce the amount of overwhelm they feel.

I'm <u>not</u> suggesting you should commit to drastically changing your family's lifestyle forever or committing you to a boring lifestyle! I am suggesting you review, reflect and notice what's going on and then carefully adapt your lifestyle, your responses, and your beliefs about how you "should" parent. And of course, this is age appropriate - it will be different for everyone depending on your child's age.

I am sharing my experience of how I started to understand my daughter's sensitivities and what I wish my Mum had done when I was a child.

It's likely that the information in this module is confirmation of your own internal thoughts and validates what you already know.

Now you know that your child is sensitive, let's dive into how we can make simple changes and become more aware of how their lifestyle can affect their sensitive nature.

When do your child's sensitivities increase and become unmanageable?
When do they become overwhelmed?

Noticing and adapting.

It could be after school, after play group, on a Sunday night after late nights and busy weekends, on a Thursday after gymnastics and swimming class, it could be after a play date or after a family gathering. It could be while at the shopping center or before a party.

Try asking your sensitive child what makes them feel more sensitive if you don't know yourself.

This kind of noticing can't be done overnight or in one weekend; especially if you have multiple children! This part is going to take time and patience. This part will still leave you frustrated and feeling hopeless. But this part may also give you your biggest breakthroughs and your biggest triumphs.

You may already know what triggers and overwhelms your child, but these might even change as they get older, so keep an open mind and heart. Once children get older and sleep overs, late nights, boyfriends/girlfriends, hormones and even alcohol gets added to the mixture, sensitivities can become a whole new ball game!

When does your child become overwhelmed? What's going on for them?

Notice, notice, notice

You might want to discuss what you notice with your spouse or a friend who has a Highly Sensitive Child too, to get another perspective. You may want to keep a journal so you can record when the overwhelm meltdown was and what was going on before or around the time.

The main thing is to keep noticing, keep being aware.

Once you know what really overwhelms your child and then when the overwhelm is likely to occur - you will be more empowered to be able to adapt your lifestyle and your responses to their behavior. Remember their behavior and sensitivities may shift as they get older.

Adapt, Adapt, Adapt

Being adaptable is a skill, and it's one I think us mothers are instantly upgraded with as soon as we give birth! Fathers - you rock too!

You can't be a parent without adapting - control and routine goes out of the window when you've experienced more spew, cr*p and Peppa Pig before 7am than most people have experienced in their whole lives.

And so, once you have noticed and noticed some more what overwhelms your child, it's time to start adapting.

- Adapting your lifestyle choices and try to be empathic to yourself and to your child.
- Adapting your reactions so they become responses.
- Adapting your views, choices and values even!

Check in with your child's timetable

Looking at your child's schedule; does it allow for free time and space, regularly and consistently? Just to do nothing? And not iPad or TV time - I mean quiet, unstimulated time to talk, play, or just sit, time?

Do you notice a correlation with busy lifestyle/weekend and sensitive related melt-downs?

Maybe your child attends a playgroup or nursery, has started school or has transitioned from primary to secondary and is struggling to cope?

I work in a range of schools & settings and can tell you - they are overwhelming!

School learning in itself is draining, couple that with processing a vast range of sensory information whilst there, it is no wonder that children of all ages struggle with their sensitive nature after a day at school.

Clubs, extracurricular activities and busy weekends are added pressure.

Of course, we want our children to learn to swim, or play sport, or attend parties, and I'm not suggesting we shouldn't give these experiences to our children.

What they do need however, is BALANCE.

Without balance (adequate rest, space and free time, alongside opportunities to socialise and learn new things) sensitives become overwhelmed and <u>won't thrive.</u>

From my own experience combined with what I have researched; we have to get our children to feel safe, secure and to a place of understanding before we can expect them to successfully undertake a range of extra-curricular and social activities and thrive at being a Highly Sensitive person in a non-sensitive world.

With this in mind, take an honest look at their lifestyle. Does your sensitive child get enough balance? Do they have time to just simply "do nothing"?

<u>Clear schedules and making time for downtime.</u>

As a first-time parent, I wanted my child to be doing what other children were doing too. I wanted her to be popular and have play dates, have lots of friends and attend parties. I wanted her to have hobbies and successes and "do" lots of stuff. I honestly just wanted to be the best parent I could be.

For some reason I thought being a good parent meant getting her to do all that stuff listed above and more! But what I came to realise is that she wasn't like all the other children, and if I pushed my wants onto her, it came at a cost - meltdowns, tantrums, frustration, crying and general unhappiness. And nothing ever turned out as I hoped it would - afternoons at Disney on Ice were a disaster for example.

To be a good parent to my sensitive daughter meant listening and understanding her needs, it meant being different and doing things differently. It meant putting my own wants and ideals aside and allowing her to find her own way, in her own time.

So, I urge you to say no, create space, and have guilt free "nothing" time. I urge you to turn the TV and the tablets off (this is a battle in my home too! But oh, so worth it!) Try dropping an extracurricular activity or a busy weekend. Leave them at home (if you can) when you go to the shops.

I will talk more about calming techniques in the next Module, but for now, just notice how busy their lifestyle is and the reasons behind this. Is there something that could be let go of?

So, what can I do?

Here are some simple adjustments we made to daily life, to help reduce sensitive overwhelm; they may or may not all be relevant to you.

- Turning the TV off at a certain time (1 hour before bed in our house - but remember for my daughter visual stimulation is what overwhelms her)
- Reducing the amount of 'noise' in the house; background noise (like a radio or the TV no one is watching) is yet another thing to process
- On days where we have parties to attend at the weekend we don't do other stuff, like attempt to go to the shopping center or see other people, we just go home and be in our own space
- Don't compare your life to the life of other people - this simple act takes the pressure of you. Know that you're being a good parent to your sensitive child. You don't need to take your sensitive child to the zoo or the soft play for them to be happy. Simplicity counts
- Find outdoor spaces that aren't full of people! There's nothing better than being in nature; but nature filled with crowds of people loses its essence and the benefits
- Setting up accessible places for them to be able to do what they love without supervision i.e. a drawing table with pencils, beanbags with books, Lego table for building and then encouraging that
Empathising with their vocalised sensitivities, rather than trying to sweep

"whinging" under the carpet or toughen her up: "OK, I can see that really hurt you, I'm very sorry you hurt yourself/your brother hit you, what will make it feel better? Rather than "Oh stop it, that didn't hurt, you're ok."
- Don't push - if they aren't ready to do something yet they will let you know. Follow their lead and know in time, that they will blossom and thrive.

This sounds all a bit boring!

While it may seem like I'm suggesting for you to commit to a boring lifestyle, full of minimal stimulation and "SPACE", I'm really not suggesting you be this stringent FOREVER!

It's merely a stage of learning and then NOTICING how giving your child this space and down time affects them. They may need very little, or they may need a lot. They might need more at certain times of their lives (transitions or busy times like Christmas) and they might not.

Some sensitive's (about 30% - Dr. Aron) are extroverts and live in busy, large, bustling families and will have already adapted to their surroundings.

I feel that because I discovered Sensitivity when my daughter was a baby, I was able to nurture her with the understanding and compassion I'm suggesting within this eBook she knows herself, that she is sensitive, and that I understand that too. I use the techniques in Module 3 and she understands why - my hope is she will use these for herself as she gets older.

Because I spent the time to get to know her sensitivities and her "flash points" I also know when she is likely to be more sensitive and overwhelmed, and so don't expect as much "good" behavior as I normally would. I ignore the outbursts and the overly sensitive reactions; giving empathy and compassion, rather than getting annoyed or frustrated! I explain these to my husband so he doesn't get annoyed with her behavior.

A word about you…

Children's sensitive overwhelm behavior can be overwhelming to deal with! So, notice what's going on for **you** at these times. Are you overwhelmed too and unable to be as understanding as maybe you'd like to be?

Notice YOUR mood when your child is being "sensitive"; are you in a "negative" mood? Feeling "off" or carrying something which is weighing you down - like guilt, resentment, unhappiness or anxiety - but pretending to your child 'everything is OK', will cause them to be confused. They will sense something is wrong - especially if they are empathic and intuitive.

As I've mentioned before, sensitive children can be empathic too; meaning they pick up on moods and the 'energy' of other people - including you.

So, if this is the case and you feel like your mood is affecting them, try telling them - "Mummy is feeling really rubbish today, it's affecting my mood and how I'm behaving, but it shouldn't and I'm sorry.

Can we do something silly and fun?" They might ask you questions, they might not - but at least you're validating their felt experience

Kathryn Pearson © 2017   www.kathrynpearson.co.uk

by telling the truth and not hiding something which inherently they can **feel** - even if you think you're masking it really well!!

Next time you're getting sucked into a sensitive meltdown, notice what's going on and why it's occurring and how you're reacting. Notice how you're feeling. Take some deep breaths and remind yourself that you're doing the best job you can, right in this moment. Think about responding to the behavior rather than reacting or getting wound up, and think about doing something to lighten your mood - asking for help, taking a dance break, locking yourself in the bathroom for a cry, spontaneously laughing or making this awful situation into a joke and just having a hug.

Getting your child to understand their own sensitive nature

From an early age (or as soon as I understood about Highly Sensitive People), I started to open the discussion with my daughter about her being sensitive too. I mainly did this so she knew that I understood her and to help equip her with the knowledge she needed when I wasn't around; so, she could start to self-manage and self-soothe her own high sensitivity.

Obviously, you should follow your own lead on this one; I'm not saying you have to talk to your child about them being sensitive. But sharing what you learn and feel comfortable with, will help your sensitive child feel less alone and more understood; which is vital for Highly Sensitive people. If you validate the fact that they are different and sensitive, it makes it OK, it makes it acceptable and it helps them feel more secure in themselves.

Follow their lead. Ask a few questions and see where it takes you.

I personally feel that if children learn about High Sensitivity from an earlier age, they can learn to self-manage overwhelm and recognise themselves when they are out of balance.

It empowers them to know they own needs and be in charge of their self-care.

"You're getting upset easily because you've had a busy day and you're sensitive, so it makes you feel funny. What we need to do is go home and have some calm and quiet time…."

Oh, how I wish my Mum would have said this to me….

Really, a Highly Sensitive person just wants to feel understood.

They want reassurance from us, their parents that they are completely normal for feeling the way they do inside - even though it's different from what everyone else can do/is like.

Kathryn Pearson © 2017   www.kathrynpearson.co.uk

We do a lot of talking. Never presume your child is too young to have what seems like a grown-up conversation to you. Sensitive children are often far more emotionally intelligent than they let on. And if you want your child to be able to come to you with their problems when they are older, you have to open the gateway NOW - or as soon as you can.

Listening to their little problems and empathising with how they feel is crucial. E.g. My daughter, at bedtime, was a little more clingy than usual. I asked her why. She came out with some rambling about how she had been challenged to run a race with some children in her class, but she didn't want to. The children continued to ask her to join in with this race but she didn't want to (fear of failure/she never wanted to in the first place/she was now playing nicely with some friends etc).

It would have been so easy to say, "Oh well, you should have just joined it, don't be silly, just ignore them next time."

But instead of sweeping this under the carpet - I asked "OK, so how did that make you feel?

Why do you feel sad (sadness in her voice) about that?"

And this is the key, I believe, to opening up that communication line, opening up that relationship, getting them to feel like you understand them, so that you're there when they need you. Building trust & opening the lines of communication.

It's hard at first for younger children to articulate and communicate how they feel.

Shrugs of the shoulders can make you think they're just making it up (and sometimes they will be, just to get that extra few mins of attention - they are after all children, and they need you more sometimes!) but try putting yourself in their shoes; how would their scenario make you feel? I suggested that the boys pestering her might have made her feel a little uneasy and that I was sorry that they had been giving her a hard time.

She then opened up and discussed little more about how she felt. I responded with empathy and gave her a little nudge "It's OK for you to feel that way; I would have felt like that too. Maybe next time you feel like that, how about trying to feel OK with saying no to people, say "NO THANK YOU I DONT WANT TO!" In a loud and proud voice and knowing that that's OK!" and we ended up making it into a joke.

It took less than 5 mins, it wasn't very taxing, but she was calmer, more confident and I instantly felt like her clinginess dissolved. She went straight to bed and sleep - no issue.

Taking the time to communicate, even when there are 101 million other things to do, even at bedtime and even when you just can't muster up the strength to, will reap benefits. Asking, listening and delving into feelings is just where the magic is.

I had no idea I was sensitive, none at all.

I was an only child, who helped with my need for space and downtime; I got it merely by being at home in the late 80's and early 90's. But as I moved through life, went to university for example, I had NO IDEA of my need for this personal space. I had no idea why I couldn't keep up with the other students. I had no idea how to manage my sensitive "neurotic" outbursts or why I had them. I had no idea how to care for myself or what my needs were.

Looking back my Mum had no idea either and I sometimes do think this has an impact on our relationship; it created a distance and a misunderstanding between us.

I couldn't explain why I was being snappy and irritable, why I was sobbing for no reason, why I would implode in tears on a Friday evening, why I couldn't just simply "ignore the mean boys at school" I couldn't explain why I felt different, I couldn't explain why I HAD to make her and my step Dad turn down the TV every night (I have supersonic hearing and the sound of the TV used to keep me awake), I couldn't explain why I only wanted to wear certain clothes (the new ones had funny seams and made me want to rip my own skin off!)

I couldn't explain why I didn't want a hobby. Thankfully now we understand each other much better! But growing up in a world where being a Highly Sensitive Person just meant you were a bit of a wimp, was horrible!

I don't want this for any more sensitive's; the loneliness the confusing, the bewildering feeling that something is wrong with you.

Sensitive's need to know that they are understood by their mothers and fathers. Sensitives need to be understood and valued within their groups and communities, their schools and then their workplaces.

Sensitivity is only a weakness when it's not understood and when it is ignored!

Kathryn Pearson © 2017   www.kathrynpearson.co.uk

Module 3
Calm, Cleanse & Protect

Module 3 Cleanse and Calm

This module delves into the practical side of parenting a Highly Sensitive. It takes a bit of effort and "doing" but if it wasn't for these techniques, I know personally, I would still be in turmoil about my sensitivity.

Using them with my daughter has been precious - I love seeing herself managing and self-regulating her emotions with her sensitive tool kit!

For me, they are my anchor as an adult. I know when I'm overwhelmed and anxious; I need some self-care (that isn't wine, chocolate and a night on the sofa).

So, it's these techniques that I turn to help keep me calm and in control.

I can't tell you how much these practices have changed my life and how I'm able to manage my sensitivity, and I hope they will be fundamental in your child's journey too.

<u>Energy</u>

One of the first things to understand when it comes to calming your child is that "things", (places and other people) are made up of energy. This "energy" can be felt, noticed and even absorbed by your sensitive child, especially if they are empathic too.

They notice more, the invisible, intangible, the unseen. Their central nervous system picks up on the delicate vibrations and energies of other people, objects and places; it can absorb it, without anyone being aware of it.

So, when they have had a busy day, birthday parties or days at school, for example, their own energy can be clogged up with this energy, and give a feeling of fuzz or tingling that contributes to their overwhelm.

I personally used to get so overwhelmed that I felt like my body was going to explode. This invisible tingling or buzzing around me was insanely disturbing; causing me to "freak out", shriek irrationally and want to shake my whole body free. I can't say this will be the same for everyone; your child may have another way of "feeling".

Before we try and calm our children (or ourselves in my case!) down, it's helpful to cleanse their energy first – but this isn't essential.

Kathryn Pearson © 2017   www.kathrynpearson.co.uk

If cleansing isn't an option (say you're out in public for example), calming techniques can be used first and cleanse later.

The cleansing techniques act as calming practices too and help to successfully "clear" the feelings you children might be contributing to their overwhelm, which in turn might calm them down. When they are combined with the calming practices, they become really powerful.

I'm sure your child will find and choose their own favorites; I've tried to include as many techniques as possible, so you have a library to choose from. I tend to mix and match my approach, and this has changed as my daughter has gotten older. Try what works for you, and refer to this guide frequently to remind yourself :)

Cleansing techniques Salt Baths

The absolute go-to is a salt bath. Salt has been used for centuries as a bathing cleansing solution. They also have a ton of health benefits too. Think of how refreshed you feel after a dip in the sea!

My favorite is Epsom salt; popping a handful into a warm bath and allowing your child to just play is as simple as it has to be.

Epsom salt is a powerful energy/auric cleanser (as well as being great for aching muscles and colds) and can literally pull away the negative energy/energies your child might have picked up.

Caution would need to be applied for very young children as they may swallow the water – Epsom salt can be used to treat constipation and can be taken internally, so with very young children this would need to be monitored.

Himalayan salt (finely ground) and magnesium salt or dead sea salt can also be used, I just personally prefer Epsom Salt as it dissolves easily and completely and just *feels* different - like you're being held, back in the womb kind of feeling!! Trust me on this one, just try it :)

Explaining to children that it is there to help them "get rid of the funny feeling or the funny energy they have picked up" should ring true to them, however explain it in any way you feel they would understand and feels comfortable:

- "Magic salt" or "calming salt" might work. Play around and adapt this for your child. Epsom salt does looks quite "crystally" so you can get away with magic salt!

If baths are a no-no and showers are the preferred option, then ask your child to imagine the shower water washing away any 'feelings' or 'negative energy they have picked up'.

- You could try a fun Epsom salt foot-bath perhaps?!
- Hand washing is great for this too. Our hands are the extensions of our hearts, and can get weighed down with energy too.

If you don't feel like you can explain, or your child is too young, just know that water and the salt is cleansing. Your intentions are just as important - a bath or a shower is a cleansing ritual. When you bathe, you wash away the "energy" from around you - it really is as simple as that.

You can add relaxing or cleansing oils to the bath too. My favorites would be Lavender and Frankincense. I use DoTerra oils (I don't sell them; I enrolled with DoTerra so that I could have access to their wholesale prices, and you can too! I can hook you up with many of my friends who sell DoTerra - see below) because of the purity and their sustainability policies. However organic oils and Neal's' yard are also fine.

I would note that some people find DoTerra expensive - this is because of the purity of the oils - 1 bottle of lavender can last me 6-9 months of everyday use and a bottle of Frankincense can last up to 18 months. However appealing cheaper oils can be, know that they can be mixed with other synthetic (fake) scents and substances, irritants and chemicals before they are sold to you. They tend not to smell pure and can irritate sensitives!

Kathryn Pearson © 2017   www.kathrynpearson.co.uk

Essential oils are not essential to help clearing & calming your sensitive child; but if you feel called to use them, please don't waste your money on awful quality, cheap oils. You want therapeutic grade oils, simple.

For more info on DoTerra see page 39 or contact me at kathrynpearsoneft@gmail.com

To Recap: a bath is a cleansing practice. Play around with what salt to use and whether you use oils. Salt baths can be a weekly practice or a daily thing - there really are no rules, working out what works best for you and your child is key.

(Tip: Places like Home Bargains, B & M and Poundland often have bath salts for sale much more cheaply than in Supermarkets or health food shops)

Cleansing & protecting Sprays

A specially made cleansing (or protection) spray can be used to clear the space around your child. Written instructions of how to do so are given below.

You can think of a cleansing or protective spray as a way of distracting attention and could be seen as a 'mental' placebo for your child.

However, I believe the ingredients we use in the spray are cleansing and have an energetic effect; cleansing the aura and subtle energy fields around your child, in a similar way to the salt bath. Having the intention that this spray will be protecting/cleansing also means the spray will carry your intention. You can also buy "Aura sprays", but I think making one is super special.

I first got the idea to make my own sprays after attending a retreat with Rebecca Campbell (Author of Light is the New Black and Rise Sister Rise), who led the group of women I was with to make a spray, and then since I have developed intuitively my own way of doing things. I highly recommend you do the same and don't rely too much on the instructions.

Just do what feels right to you and don't take it too seriously - your intention is all that really matters.

What you need:

- A water spray bottle

- Small amount of salt e.g. 1 level teaspoon (Himalayan or Epsom)

- Essential oils such as lavender, sage, basil, frankincense - any others that appeal

- Small crystal (such as rose quartz, clear quartz, amethyst or any crystal your child is drawn to) - optional

- Natural water (sea water, spring water, stream water) if you can't, tap water can still be used.

What to do:

1. Collect your natural water and sit it in a bowl or a jug

2. Place your crystal in the water and ask the crystal to release its gentle energy into the water for the protection or cleansing of your child (you can ask in any way you like!)

3. It it happens to be a full moon, place your water outside under the moon light and ask that the moon light infuses the water with cleansing or protective energy, to help your child - name them.

4. In the morning collect the water, remove the crystal and dissolve the salt within the water. (salt used for cleansing, if making a protective spray this can be omitted)

5. Transfer the water into the spray bottle and add 5-10 drops of your chosen essential oils (this part is optional)

6. Seal and label and add any further intentions to it.

Use the spray whenever you feel like your child needs it or asks for it.

Introduce them to the spray beforehand, tell them what it does and why. Tell them you made it or that you bought it - be as authentic as possible. Believe in it and they will too.

My daughter asks for her spray before she goes to school if she is feeling wobbly or tired (extra sensitive) or if she knows she will have to see/be with certain people. We keep it by the door so we don't forget, but you could keep one in the car or your handbag for emergencies!

I typed "Aura Sprays UK" into Google Shopping and got 100's of results. There are many on the market if you don't have the time to make one yourself, ranging from a few quid to £10.

If you fancy a splurge, I highly recommend Aura Soma.

You can buy from a UK supplier here: www.11essence.co.uk. The Pink or White Air Conditioner
Sprays would be perfect as a room spray for your child.

Or using the Pink or White Pomanders as an Aura treat.

If you'd like to ask me about these please get in touch - kathrynpearsoneft@gmail.com

Sage/Palo Santo

Burning White Sage bundles, Palo Santo and Incense has been used for centuries for cleansing spaces and energy fields. I love Sage; however, my family does not! It can be a bit smelly. However, I cleanse our home regularly and after we have had visitors.

I also Sage myself before a Salt Bath for extra cleansing results.

Why Sage?
The smoke from dried sage actually changes the ionic composition of the air and space around us - so our aura for example can be cleansed powerfully by using sage, and can have a direct effect on reducing our stress response.

You can read more at Mind Body Green. *(https://www.mindbodygreen.com/0-17875/a-sage-smudging-ritual-to-cleanse-your-aura-clear-your-space.html)*

Directions to use Sage

You can buy a bundle (these are most popular) or loose leaf white sage from health food/spiritual shops or online.

When you want to cleanse your home or your child's "space" then light the end of the bundle or the leaf. Allow the smoke to drift. Traditionally a feather is used to 'waft' the smoke around the space or person. However, I tend to use my hand or a small book!

Kathryn Pearson © 2017   www.kathrynpearson.co.uk

Move around the house with the intention of cleansing the energy field of the house/room.

You can also cleanse your/your child's aura by wafting the smoke around your/their bodies.

Please take extra care here! There is a fire hazard and a risk or burning yourself/your child.

Why Palo Santo?

Its name literally means "holy wood", and it is just that. When it is burned, the smoke is believed to have both medicinal and therapeutic healing power.

Traditionally, it is burned by Incas, indigenous people of the Andes, Shamans and medicine people for spiritual purifying, energy cleansing and healing.

You can read more (http://www.energymuse.com/blog/palo-santo-uses/)

Palo Santo in general, does a similar job to sage, but it smells nicer! It can be slightly harder to come by, but you can still easily buy online. You use it in the same way as sage.

I personally prefer the spray and salt bath option with children, just because they don't involve fire or smelly smoke - which could be hazardous around children. I love cleansing smokes for myself, and keep these as rituals for myself and one my daughter might take up as she gets older.

Crystals

You can also ask crystals to cleanse spaces for you. I really am no crystal expert; my favorite crystal expert is a friend Katie, at "Crystal Muse" on Instagram. Tell her I sent you. Visit here >>> www.crystalmuse.co.uk <<<

However, I do have the knowledge to be able to get you started.

There are many crystals that would be great for clearing spaces, such as clear or Smokey quartz, rose quartz, amethyst, obsidian. I personally use a big chuck of selenite that I have, to clear spaces. I also keep tumble stones of my favorite crystals in bowls around the house.

What to do:

Technique adapted from "Learn Lemurian Healing" by Tiffany Wardle.

Again, intention is essential.

1.   Firstly, cleanse the crystal in natural water, such as a stream, sea water or lake. If not possible dissolve some salt in a bowl of water and set them in that for 5-10 mins (do check this is ok with the type of crystal you have, as not all can sit in water) Again, if this is too much hassle; running tap water and your intention works just as well. Just hold the

crystal under the water with the intention of cleansing it.

2. Wash and cleanse the crystal by holding the intention to cleanse the crystal of any negative energy it has picked up or absorbed, imagine the water washing them away and down the plug hole/back out to sea.

3. See the energy dissipating or dispersing and eventually being absorbed by the earth, which transmutes and recycles this energy. Thank the earth and the water for their part in this process.

4. Next get comfy and hold the crystal in your left hand and imagine the crystal being surrounded by a bright white light for a few moments.

5. Then in your mind, ask the crystal to clear and absorb the negative energy from the space around you/your home/your child.

6. Create and hold the vision of the crystal clearing the space and what it would be like afterwards. You might visualise a white light emanating out from the crystal or travelling around the room, clearing as it goes. If you find this tricky in the beginning, you can simply say over and over in your mind "please clear and cleanse the space around ***" until you feel you are 'done'.

Kathryn Pearson © 2017   www.kathrynpearson.co.uk

7.   Hold this for a few minutes, or until you feel you are 'done', then cup your right hand over left and it is complete!

8.   Place the crystal in the space you want clearing and let it do its thing - in your child's bedroom maybe, or a family room. After a day or two, cleanse the crystal again and repeat the process, (maintenance approach) or you may just want to do this when the feelings get too heavy, and it's obvious the space needs clearing, (emergency approach!)

Calming Techniques

The Epsom salt bath, suggested earlier, can be used a calming technique as well as a cleansing technique. Really, it's my go to after a long day to avoid overwhelm at bed time.

So, I have selected and outlined my favorite quick and easy calming techniques below. Please note: they may not work with your child; they may also need introducing to your child before melt down occurs and practicing before being successful. Please be playful, experimental, adaptable and patient!

Breathing techniques

Breathing has become a bit of an obsession for me; teaching breathing practices in both my day jobs (Teaching <u>Teen Yoga</u> & with <u>Each Amazing Breath</u>) has meant I'm a little over passionate about them!

Calm and attentive breathing has been shown to calm the sympathetic (stress) nervous system - so really good for calming down. Deep, diaphragmatic (Tummy) breathing actually activates the relaxation response within the body, and over time, creates a

calmer and more self-aware "you" - which is great for younger children to learn now; imagine your child being able to self regulate and control their emotions!

Being more self-aware allows us humans to better understand and know our own needs; which helps us care for ourselves better.

Excerpt adapted from: Take Five At School: Quantitive and Qualitative Report on the Impact of 'Take Five' at School; An analysis of the impact on a Year 6 class at Worksop Priory CE Primary School (2015) For More information about Take Five C visit here:*wwweachamazingbreath.org*

Amazing, right?

Teaching them to notice and use their breathing to calm down is such an important life-long skill.

So how can we do this? With my daughter I firstly assessed how aware of her breath she was (aged about 3/4) by asking her to breathe in and out a few times. Usually with younger children they deep breaths and gulp in air; and blow out hard - your child may or not be like this. She took in deep breaths, held it in and let it out quite quickly; so from this point I worked on slowing her breath down and making it gentler.

How to develop slow and gentle breathing:

Practical Technique adapted from: Julie Christian; Yoga Teacher, Mentor and Each Amazing Breath Trainer.

*Find Julie on Facebook -
http://www.facebook.com/julesinyoga*

Ask your child to breathe in and imagine smelling a flower, or a cake, or a bowl of soup for example, by cupping their hands in front of them. Then ask them to breathe out by gently blowing out as if they were gently blowing a candle out.

Keep trying this at different times, and know they will build upon each experience. You're aiming for a gentle and calm in breath, with a slow, gentle and calm out breath. It might not happen immediately!

Another and practical way is to actually get some flower petals or a feather (or something else light) and cup them in their hands. Show them how to gently "smell" and breathe in and then gently blow away the petals or the feather, but not in one go!

Challenge them to breathe out but not blow all the petals or feathers off in one go - they will eventually learn how to breathe out gently and slowly.

Now work this practice into life - in the car, before bedtime, whenever suits! Make it fun and non-pressured. Once your child has mastered being able to breathe in and out gently - noticing their breath - you will be able to use it as a calming technique when your child is fractious or at sensitive times.

Kathryn Pearson © 2017   www.kathrynpearson.co.uk

You've probably told your child to take a deep breath, when they are fractious, anxious or upset; but have you ever taught them this? People, in general, don't think that they need to learn how to breathe, or focus on their breath, because they do it all the time! The act of breathing in and out is automatic; the body does it for us, but it's the only automatic system of the body which we can actively control too.

When I read 'The Science of Breath', I shifted. I realised and saw the breath as the important process it is. It acts a bridge between the mind and the body.

The mind sends signals to the body via the breath, usually in the form of a quickening or shallowing of the breath when faced with panic, fear or sadness - notice how your own breath changes when these emotional reactions occur.

However, we can calm these reactions by noticing (being aware of) and controlling the breath. It really is so important, and I would highly recommend you take some time to teach your child calm, attentive breathing.

To read more about this topic I recommend: The Science of Breath By Rama Swami

Grounding
What is grounding?

Getting your child to notice the floor beneath them can be an amazing way of calming them down! In Teen Yoga we use it all the time in Mountain pose or tree pose, as a way of taking our thoughts from our head (which usually distract us!) and down to our feet, helping us feel stronger and more stable and literally 'rooted' into the ground. I like to use it with my daughter when she feels unsafe or is excessively worried or in pain.

The online Physics Classroom writes: "Grounding is the process of removing the excess charge of an object by means of the transfer of electrons between it and another object of substantial size. When a charged object is grounded, the excess charge is balanced by the transfer of electrons between the charged object and the ground".

> "For people, grounding literally removes the excess energies of stress and anxiety…"
> *Take Five At School: Quantitive and Qualitative Report on the Impact of 'Take Five' at School; An analysis of the impact on a Year 6 class at Worksop Priory CE Primary School (2015)*

You could think of it as you are letting go of 'negative' energy, such as stress and worry, by transferring it into the ground.

Kathryn Pearson © 2017   www.kathrynpearson.co.uk

Grounding can be as simple as noticing the floor/chair/bed beneath you. You can build upon this practice by pushing unwanted feelings or emotions out through your feet or out with the breath, or connecting into the ground with roots, like a tree or a plant would, and allowing unwanted feelings out via these roots.

How to do it

This technique has been developed from my work and teachings both with Each Amazing Breath and Teen Yoga.

When your child is getting frustrated, worried or stressed, simply ask them to feel the floor underneath them and do their calm breathing, while taking all their attention down to their feet. You can do this lying down by asking them to notice where their body is touching the ground/bed.

You could ask them imagine they are growing roots into the ground through their feet or you could ask them to breathe out stress or worry by imagining it going out through their feet and into the ground, or leaving their body through their breath/roots.

Again grounding, as well as breathing, is a key tool that a Highly Sensitive person can feel more in control and calm themselves down. Once learned, it can be done anywhere.

Kathryn Pearson © 2017   www.kathrynpearson.co.uk

Hand Mudra Technique

I was taught this Mudra (hand movement/position) and mantra (chant) during my <u>Teen Yoga</u> *training.*

I found my daughter struggled with this at first; as her manual dexterity wasn't developed enough. However, she practiced it and finally nailed it and I have found it works very well with older children; stick with it and don't give up; sometimes my daughter is TOO frustrated to do this technique; it's too challenging for her to do when she's upset, so just bear that in mind too.

Sitting comfortably, hands on knees with palms facing up, touch each fingertip in turn (starting with the index through to the little) with the tip of the thumb.

When you touch the thumb to the index finger say "Peace"
When you touch the thumb to the middle finger say "Begins"
When you touch the thumb to the ring finger say "With"
When you touch the thumb to the little finger say "Me"

You can teach children to do this with one hand or both hands and teach them to breathe in and out slowly/deeply/calmly.

Kathryn Pearson © 2017   www.kathrynpearson.co.uk

It takes a certain amount of focus and concentration to do this and so may distract your child when they are feeling overwhelmed, worried or anxious.

You might find that the phrase "peace begins with me" means nothing to your child, so you could adapt it so it means something to them like "*their name* is calming down", i.e. "Freddie is calming down".

Relaxing Body Scan

If you've ever been to a yoga class, you will know how special and lovely the end of the class - the lying down part!

And one particular fractious night, my daughter was really struggling to settle down to go to sleep. In my frustration I thought "I am able to relax and literally put to sleep teenagers week after week; why can't I do the same for my daughter?" A little voice whispered back "You can!"

So, I just started to ask her to relax her body parts, as I do during my teen yoga classes during the relation part of the class. And before I knew it she was lying still and quiet and I was able to leave the room within a few minutes.

A Body Scan is a simple way of focusing your attention on each body part in turn and consciously relaxing it. In Yoga you would do a deeper Yoga Nidra practice, but I find that the simple body scan explained below, is enough for younger children.

I've recorded an audio guide for you below to help you learn what to say which can be found here: http://www.kathrynpearson.co.uk/calm-clear-for-sensitive-children/

Worry monster and Fairy doors

These things are widely available in the shops, and you're likely to already have at least one in the home. A Google search will hook you up to these products. We have the fairy doors and often write worries and problems to our fairy and she magically helps or has some words of wisdom for my daughter in the morning.

I love the idea of a worry monster too. I wish I had had one of these when I was younger. If your child is a worrier or very anxious, then I would say give these a try. The act of writing your problems down is so helpful. Sometimes as a sensitive the thoughts and worries in our heads can build up and become too much to handle - causing overwhelm. Getting the problems out of their heads and onto paper is such a help sometimes.

Essential Oils

As I've mentioned before, I use essential oils to help calm my daughter down. Lavender,

Frankincense and a DoTerra blend called Serenity are my favorites.

I find them exceptional. They smell divine; they're completely natural and safe and really, really work for us.

I diffuse them. I put them in baths. I mix them with a carrier cream or oil (like fractionated coconut oil (or just normal coconut oil if I'm short on the fractionated stuff!)) and rub them onto my daughter's spine and feet.

Dr Laura Hughes, whom I met on a retreat in Glastonbury this year, is possibly my favorite go-to lady about why we should use essential oils. You can find her low down here > http://www.drlaurahughes.com/introductionessential-oils/

Having a good cry

Sensitive people and children especially, due to their developmental stage, are emotional and often their emotions are close to the surface. Sometimes a good cry is essential to "let go", and nurture that it's OK not to be OK and happy all the time.

Protection Techniques

If you or your child are Sensitive and Empaths, then you will certainly benefit from some protection. Empaths seem to "absorb" the energies of others. This was the trait that I struggled with the most my whole life. I never really knew how I felt because I spent all my time feeling other people's energies or collective energies I had 'picked up'.

For example; if I went to meet a friend and they were in a funny mood, or someone was overly stressed at work, how I would feel would change, once I was in their presence.

Their mood, their "energy" would affect my mood, my "energy". Similarly, I found I was so sensitive & empathic that those 'collective' energies would affect me too.

So, if something big was happening in the world, such as a natural disaster or Political outrage or public demonstrations (Women marching against Trump for example) I got affected too; through unexplained feelings of hopelessness, anger or tears for no reason. I felt weak and hopeless most of the time. Unable to own my emotions or even get to know them, so that I could take care of my own needs.

Protection techniques probably strengthened me the most, but I still struggle to get it right now. I've listed some of the ways I protect my energy (or should do); again, I suggest an experimental approach and patience.

<u>Crystals</u>

First of all, I use crystals. I haven't quite managed to perfect this with my daughter yet, as I don't feel she is old enough to carry crystals with her. But there are people who make simple crystal jewellery for children (Etsy, Instagram etc) in the form of bead bracelets and such. If you feel called to use crystals please do! I certainly believe protective crystals were a huge turning point for me and I believe in the power of them!

My favorite protective & grounding crystals are Jet, Tigers Eye, Hematite, Labradorite, Smoky Quartz, Black Onyx, Amethyst or Black Tourmaline.

I carry a piece of Jet on me at all times; I find it to be a gentle stone, which carries protective qualities. I used to have black tourmaline, a turquoise ring and obsidian! But the combination of the 3 made me a bit overwhelmed sometimes, so now I just use the Jet. My daughter loves stones and crystals and if you get the chance to take your child to a crystal shop, do it!!! Let them pick the stones they are most drawn to, keep them in a safe place and let them play around with them. Please caution that crystals could pose a choking hazard and small children should not be allowed access to small stones. Please be mindful.

You can "programme" the crystal in the same way as suggested earlier, by cleansing the crystal and then holding it in your left hand and asking it to protect ….., then holding this vision (maybe your child surrounded by protective light or shields) until you feel "done".

Older children could carry crystals and stones with them for protection and you can even teach this simple programming technique to your children so they can do it themselves.

Protective sprays

Just like the cleansing spray I mentioned before, you can make a spray to be protective too. Just ask the crystal to infuse the water with protective energy or choose crystal which are protective.

Choose oils such as Frankincense, Lavender, Cedarwood, Clary Sage, Basil.

Make your spray in the same way I instructed you to make the cleansing one, or buy one if it's easier, again I did a Google search and found loads ranging from £8-£20++

Again, if you fancied a splurge, you could visit the 11essence site to purchase Aura Soma sprays or Pomanders. Introduce them to your child before using and tell them the spray will protect them from the energy they pick up.

Invoking a protection bubble

It doesn't have to a bubble; in our house we invoke (or ask) protective Angels, lights and even fire dragons or unicorns to help protect us!

We can't be with our children all the time, and so what I decided to do was introduce different "energies" to my daughter that she could invoke (ask) them to protect her when she was alone.

A light, a bubble, an angel (Archangel Michael to be exact), a colour (Blue is associated with Archangel Michael), Fire Dragons and Unicorns can all be introduced to your child - whatever you feel comfortable with!

Tell them that whenever they feel attacked, alone or scared they can ask in their heads/minds for one of those "energies" to come and help protect them. Teach them to visualise it for themselves and see how it goes - see below for more detail.

Visualisation

You can teach your child a simple visualisation to help them do this. Ask them to close their eyes and imagine a blue (or a colour of their choosing) ball of light in front of them. Ask them to see the ball getting bigger and bigger and as it gets bigger, it starts to surround them.

Tell them that the light is strong and protective and nothing but love can get through the light. The age of your child will determine the length of this visualisation. Just play around and be patient! Try unicorns, fire/water/earth/air dragons or angels and see what works best.

But what if...?

Don't worry if your child appears not to "get" any of the techniques, or even thinks your bonkers! They might be showing some resistance to this "new approach" and resistance is good!

Stick at it - keep doing what you believe in. Keep trying and then try again. Do what feels right and what feels comfortable. You might only ever use one technique from this whole chapter - but that one technique could be life changing!

Don't let a bit of resistance to something new, put you off. I wholeheartedly believe you bought this eBook for a reason, and that reason won't always be crystal clear right away. But I trust anyway.

My daughter knows I'm not like other mum's, she knows not all children are like her and this has benefits and its pitfalls. But I stay rooted in what I believe in: Sensitives are here to save the world! Sensitives need compassion and understanding, and they need to know who they are and why they are like they are! The need to know how special they are and what their super power is.

They need to use these (or similar) techniques to calm and clear so that they can thrive in this modern world!

They might seem simple and "woo woo" and they *are.* I healed my empathic and sensitive nature with these techniques so that I could thrive as a sensitive in a modern world. All I want now is for more people to integrate these simple, natural, medicinal techniques into their lives so they can too.

Module 4
Empower & Thrive

Kathryn Pearson © 2017   www.kathrynpearson.co.uk

Empower

"Make (someone) stronger and more confident, especially in controlling their life and claiming their rights."

Oxford English Dictionary definition of 'empower'.

And so, this chapter is my last motivating talk to you, the parent of a Highly Sensitive, (Empathic and likely Intuitive AMAZING child,) to encourage you to **allow** them to be who they are, to help you to **enable** them, give them **permission** and say **it's OK** for them to be a thriving Highly Sensitive child and person.

I believe it's your task, your mission, to be their bacon of light, helping them navigate their way home to their true self.

Don't see it as a weakness!!

There's no doubt that you love your child and think they're utterly amazing. However, there may be a part of you (or a part of someone else who might be influential in your life) who thinks that being "sensitive" is a weakness.

I've been there and had the thoughts myself, and sometimes wished that my daughter was more tough and resilient like some of the other children at her school. I've worried she will struggle to fit in, I've worried people will see her as weak and treat her so. I've worried that she herself, will feel the same way I did, and believe something is wrong with her.

But I always come back to my core beliefs around this - Sensitive people are here for a reason. And once sensitivity is understood it can open doors to thriving in the world as a sensitive.

Also, I've realised my child is not me. She isn't destined to have the same experiences as I did. She's already stronger and more resilient that I ever was as a child!

Remember what I quoted in module 2 - the story of the deer? Both deer are needed for the species to survive. BOTH. There is no right or wrong way to be in life.

Some people are sensitive, and some are not and that's ok.

It's not a weakness and the world needs your sensitive child. Hold the belief that they will do something amazing for this planet and humanity and give them the confidence to make it so.

Kathryn Pearson © 2017   www.kathrynpearson.co.uk

"Darling, you're sensitive and that's OK, good, great even! You're here to do something amazing and I want to help you to find out what that is."

To the people in your life who see sensitivity as a weakness; they likely will always see it this way. But you have the knowledge, the tools and the support to educate these people and help shape or change their beliefs.

Owning sensitivity

So, having said that, it's now down to you to make your child feel as though their own sensitive uniqueness and quirks are special, are amazing and are needed in the world! It's time to stop trying to toughen our children up to survive this world, and "fit in". We no longer should have to bend and break to fit into what society has created. We no longer need to feel not good enough, weaker or less than.

I frigging own my sensitivity and wear my heart on my sleeve - quite literally!

And it has been the best decision ever. Not everyone has liked it - but mostly my friends have rejoiced in finally understanding me, my husband now "gets it" and most importantly - I OWN who I am. I know my sensitive superpower and I use it every day.

I removed myself from teaching because my sensitive body and mind couldn't take it anymore and created a life where my sensitivity is freaking celebrated (Yes, I have a boss who allows me to have time off when I'm overwhelmed and pushes me to look after myself! *She only employed my because I have the ability to be empathic and sensitive!* I also spend the rest of my time my own boss and therefore can nurture myself).

Getting your child to own their sensitivity is going to take time, and be a lifelong journey. But it starts with you celebrating and nurturing their sensitivity and their nature, now. It means being positive about their differences and making it OK to be sensitive.

Your language and what you say to them is really, really important. Your own core beliefs around sensitivity need to be authentic or they will sense it. You need to believe it too!!

The good news is that society IS changing. I've copied this exert from a video Heidi Sawyer posted on YouTube back in 2016. The link to the video can be found below. I HIGHLY recommend you watch it:

Published on Aug 26, 2016

"The world is changing. We've seen more developments in the last 15 years than in the previous 100, because of huge advances in technology. Those changes are set to continue, and as a species we're having to adapt faster than evolution allows.
But no matter what technology demands of us tomorrow and no matter how advanced it becomes, it will never be able to truly understand human empathy.

The change has already begun – it's happening now. Around the world, senior people in organisations are seeking employees with a unique skill: one that can't be outsourced to countries with a cheaper labor force or automated. It's a skill that's natural to all Intuitive-Sensitives, and one that will be in huge demand, much sooner than any of us can predict. If you've ever voiced your concerns at work but had them dismissed, only to find that time proved you right and on the next occasion all heads turned to you (even though you may not be in a position of 'authority'), then this is set to continue.

True authority isn't handed down by those in power – it's given by the collective to those who deserve it. Intuitive-Sensitives are the secret leaders, and in perhaps only a few years from now, they will no longer be hidden, or silent."

Kathryn Pearson © 2017   www.kathrynpearson.co.uk

Video Link: https://youtu.be/WElV8mP-qW4 - How Work / Life Balance will look in 2030 and

Where you Fit in as an Intuitive-Sensitive - Heidi Sawyer.

I truly believe we are at the forefront of changing perceptions and beliefs around sensitivity, especially in children. Think of us as a kind of army, leading the way and fighting (peacefully) for change! I'm so proud and happy you are here with me.

Sensitive superpower

What makes us different makes us powerful. As I have mentioned before, each Sensitive person has their own unique "fingerprint" of sensitivity, meaning not all sensitives are the same, and each one of us will carry our own unique gift - or sensitive superpower.

I've mentioned before how mine is my ability to feel, which I apply in my teaching role and my daughters is her ability to observe the details. How she will use this, we are yet to find out, but I don't ever discourage her from "observing" or make fun of her for 'knowing all the details'.

I celebrate it and tell her how amazing it is that she can do what she can do.

I hope that over time, this builds her confidence and her sense of herself and she's never ashamed or embarrassed of her "gifts".

Finding out what your child's sensitive superpower is might take a while and a lot of observing and noting yourself. They might already be naturally "gifted" at something - I can think of a family member of mine who's drawing and inventing skills are super advanced for his age and another family friend whose child is super gifted at communication. But your child's may be less obvious, like mine.

However, just KNOWING that they have a sensitive superpower means you're likely to be looking out for it and more likely to help them nurture it! So even if you don't know, just know that by reading this you are doing the most you can do right now.

Talk to your child about it

As mentioned in the previous module, talking to your child about sensitivity, for me, is crucial. Maybe your child isn't quite old enough, or there is work to be done around your own beliefs, BEFORE you talk to them. This is something that I will be talking about in the Facebook group, and which I am keen to talk openly about.

But any aspect of this book which you feel you can talk to your child about - then DO IT!

Kathryn Pearson © 2017   www.kathrynpearson.co.uk

Thrive

So how do we get our children to THRIVE in a world that is so obviously (right now) non-sensitive?

It's a multi-layered response; lots of different stuff has to be in place for a child to thrive as a sensitive. And we can create all this stuff, and then life happens, set-backs occur and we get knocked off our perch.

What I do know is that a sensitive will thrive when:

- they know/understand themselves
- they understand how to self-manage their emotions and have access to the materials needed (salt, sprays, crystals etc) - they feel confident and secure in themselves - they aren't overwhelmed (cleanse and calm) - they know they are normal - just sensitive!

My hope is that by you applying some of the things I have talked about in this eBook, and then this will enable your child to thrive.

I purposely haven't gone into detail in this chapter for two reasons:

1. I don't have all the answers!

2. I feel like a tailored approach to each individual is needed. There is no "one size fits all" answer. And finding your own path is the way.

Hobbies + Opportunities

Everyone wants their children to experience things and "be good" at something, have hobbies and opportunities. I read so much about children who really struggle with clubs and hobbies - being left alone, new people, strange environments - all can contribute to this. But for me, if a child is experiencing difficulty in attending a club, they are likely simply not ready.

This doesn't mean they won't ever be ready, but just not now, in this moment. Give them time!! If your child is school age, then know that for some sensitives, school can be enough! They don't necessarily need, or can cope with, something else.

Don't compare your child's abilities to handle stuff with someone else. There is no pressure - only the perceived pressure of other people's expectations!

Communication

Clear communication comes from mutual respect and the ability and willingness to listen to one another. I will hold my hands up and admit I'm shit at this sometimes! Utter shit!

When I'm busy and have 1 million things on my mind, listening to my daughter can be tough. It takes time and patience. But I want her to listen to me! So, I must leave that gate open, I must listen to her, especially if I want her to talk to me and listen to me!

When I surveyed parents of sensitive children, most said they wanted their child to be a bale to talk to them. Hopefully I have made my point earlier on in the book, but if you missed it - sensitive people just want to feel understood. They need you on their team, they want to talk to you, but if they feel as though their sensitivity is "bad" they may feel less inclined to speak to you about it.

Becoming 'emotionally literate' also will help this - discus emotions and how things feel, don't be afraid to go there! Ask about how things make or made them feel.

Talk to them about things that have happened to you in the past; they see you as this amazing person who handles everything, but knowing that sometimes Mummy cries in the bath because Cheryl at work was a cow today, shows them that they're not alone and you can empathise and understand them!!

Kathryn Pearson © 2017   www.kathrynpearson.co.uk

Final Word!

So, having said all of this (and I've said an awful lot!) I'd now like to give you the opportunity to do some reflection yourself. In the pages below, I give yourself the opportunity to think about and reflect on the things you can do, say, cut out, encourage in YOUR child.

I'm no Guru; I firmly believe we are our own Guru's and all the answers are inside you. I hope I've held your hand enough for you to feel confident enough to figure the rest out for yourself and find YOUR own way for your own children. I really do want to stress that these are MY experiences and some of my opinions and beliefs, (some have been divinely gifted to me, I'd like to add!!) some you may agree with and some you may not, some things might be more relevant to you than others, and some stuff might just be so bang on the nail, it's spooky.

Whatever it is, I really do encourage you to feel and test out your own way, your own path. The path that is best for you and your children. I never in a million years thought I'd write this book - a book for bloody parents?!!? Are you KIDDING me!? NEVER. But I have and I'm so pleased I have. Please get in touch if you want to chat about anything or work with me further.

So much love, always Kathy xxx

The Future

I have created a Facebook group! Search for "The Sensitive Subject" where I'll be posting videos and discussions around the topics of this eBook and I'm also there and happy to answer your questions. Please come and join us :)

The next book - "Self-Care for sensitive parents" – is one I am writing for myself. It's one I feel is so needed, right?

I hope to see you in my group and connect with you there.

For now, take a virtual hug from me as I thank you for spending this time with me and my words. I hope my words have helped you - even if it only a bit! Be proud and go empower!!

Guidance sessions

I will be offering space for a limited number of 1-2-1 guidance sessions, for parents of sensitive children. To work through specific issues or problems and tailor an approach which is completely right for you and your child. Please get in touch for more information kathrynpearsoneft@gmail.com

Other Resources

I have included some of my old YouTube video links for you to browse, if you're a

YouTube watcher! I hope to add some more soon, so please subscribe to my KATHRYN PEARSON channel for updates.

https://youtu.be/WSpEeT1tp5A - Protection for Highly Sensitive Teens (anyone basically!)

https://youtu.be/Ah1ffFogaLU - Signs of Being Highly Sensitive

https://youtu.be/-x-E1Uka8w8 - Managing your Emotions as a Highly Sensitive

I am a certified and qualified Teen Yoga teacher, currently working in South Yorkshire; I am also a level 2 Emotional Freedom technique (EFT/Tapping) practitioner - If you would like to know more about either of these services please contact me.

Kathryn Pearson © 2017   www.kathrynpearson.co.uk

Reflection Questions:

What do I believe about Sensitivity? How does it make me feel?

If you have negative beliefs about sensitivity, where do these come from?

Who or what made you believe this?

What could you do to change these beliefs?

How can you encourage your child to own their sensitive nature more?

What do you think your child's Sensitive superpower is?

What signs or behaviors make you think this?

What can you do to encourage this superpower?

What actions? What language?

Do you talk to your child about emotions and feelings?

If you don't, why do you think this is?

What's standing in your way? How could you overcome this?

Printed in Great Britain
by Amazon